*photograph by Virginia Hamilton*

Arnold Adoff, noted poet/anthologist, was born in New York City. Educated at the City College of New York, Columbia University, and the New School for Social Research, he worked for twelve years in the New York City public schools as a teacher and counselor, and he taught at New York University and Connecticut College. Mr. Adoff has edited numerous anthologies of contemporary literature and poetry, and is the author of many highly-acclaimed poetry/picture books, including *Black is Brown is Tan*, *Big Sister Tells Me That I'm Black*, *MA nDA LA*, and *Make a Circle Keep Us In*. He currently pursues his culinary interests in Yellow Springs, Ohio, where he lives with his wife, author Virginia Hamilton, and two children, Leigh Hamilton and Jaime Levi.

Lothrop, Lee & Shepard Books
New York

ISBN 0-688-41901-1
ISBN 0-688-51901-6 (lib. bdg.)

# EATS

Recipe For Eats Poems

Take One Grandma Ida in a warm kitchen smelling
        of Russian Coffee Cake and Gorky
add    One Mother Rita in a warm kitchen smelling
        of French Toast and Maupassant
combine
with  One Wife Virginia
                        in a warm kitchen smelling
        of Plum Sauce and Gertrude Stein
season
with  Two Children Jaime and Leigh
                        in a warm kitchen smelling
        of Brown Bread and Milne
place
inside A Poet$_s$ head and cook for a long time
then
serve with the enthusiasm of An Editor Dorothy
        to hungry Readers ready for the taste

Eats

     are on my mind    from early morning
       to late at night
                   in spring
                   or winter
    there is
       no wrong
       or right
         time
       to feel that sudden
              need
       to find that sudden
              meal

    i am always hungry

Not Me But

cows walk up and beg to
be
burgers
chicken legs
will tap dance
to
my
teeth
and
oatmeal cookies
have
been
known
to fly
out of their jars
as i pass by

My Mouth

        stays shut
                but
food   just
finds
      a way

              my tongue says
we are
          full today
          but
                teeth just
                      grin
              and
              s a y
                come in

i am always hungry

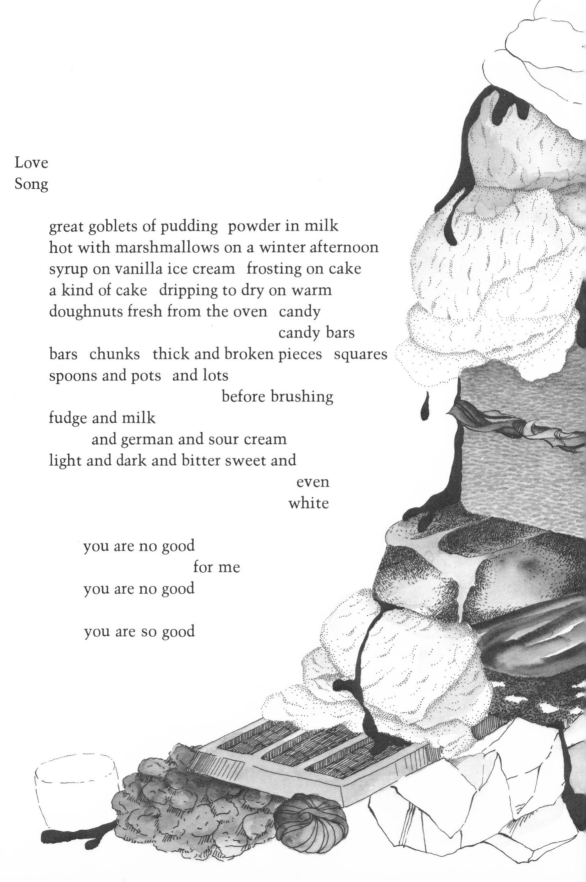

Love
Song

　　great goblets of pudding　powder in milk
　　hot with marshmallows on a winter afternoon
　　syrup on vanilla ice cream　frosting on cake
　　a kind of cake　dripping to dry on warm
　　doughnuts fresh from the oven　candy
　　　　　　　　　　　　　　candy bars
　　bars　chunks　thick and broken pieces　squares
　　spoons and pots　and lots
　　　　　　　　　　　　before brushing
　　fudge and milk
　　　　and german and sour cream
　　light and dark and bitter sweet and
　　　　　　　　　　　　　　even
　　　　　　　　　　　　　　white

　　　you are no good
　　　　　　　　　for me
　　　you are no good

　　　you are so good

Chocolate
Chocolate

       i
love
   you so
      i
want
   to
marry
   you
   and
live
   forever
     in the
      flavor
of your
  brown

Measuring and Mixing

i am
beating
breakfast
by
myself

only
assisted
        by
one
sleepy
and
older
    sister

    waiting
        for
        an
accident

As Long As

              she helps
                 me
at the stove
              with the
             low
            flame
my french
        toast
is   always
      better  browning
            in
           the
     butter

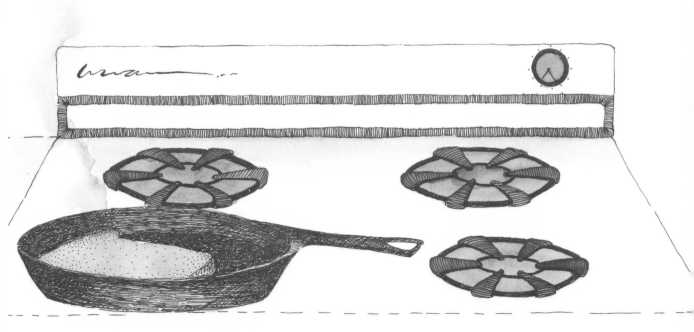

Sunday Morning Toast

in a bowl   beat 2 eggs
with ½ cup milk
a pinch of salt
½ teaspoon vanilla

dip 4 pieces of white bread   one at a time
into this mix   and when the
bread
is soaked through
it is ready to go
into
a hot and buttered skillet
or pan

then brown both sides until fluffy and done
and sprinkle with powdered sugar   or drip
honey
or maple syrup   then eat

makes enough to fill one sister and one cook
and one sunday morning boast

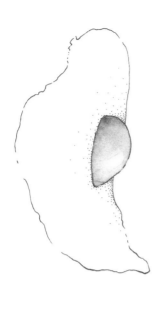

Sunny

    side
       up
    bull$_s$

    eye
    egg

    turn

    over
    easy
       and
    don$_t$ bre$_{ak}$

    the
    yoke

Only The Onions

                    are first
even before
the
last frost         into the
                        ground
                    they
                        go

to grow
 a green
   fence around the
                    cabbage
     and the lettuce
     and the beans

they will keep
                the hungry
                    young
                    rabbits

                        out

After All The Digging

              and the planting
              and the  pulling
of weeds
     on hot summer afternoons

there are cool mornings
we can
      walk between
the rows
     and bite a bean   or chew a lettuce
                        leaf
     and taste the ripe tomatoes
the
way
the rabbits
       take
  breakfast

Getting The Sweet

                        strawberries
from my
fingers
        down
        into the basket
without
            eating all of them
                            up
                            is
        the problem

        the solution
                    is
                    not
          to solve
          the problem
until
      you
        are
      full
        of answers

The Apple

is on the top
branch
of the tree
touching
the
sky
or the apple is
in
the
sky
touching
the top branch
of the tree

and i am
me on the ground
waiting
for
a
good
wind

Take One Apple

wash and
dry
and
eat
it   up and down
and side
ways
to
the
core

then
take

one
apple
more

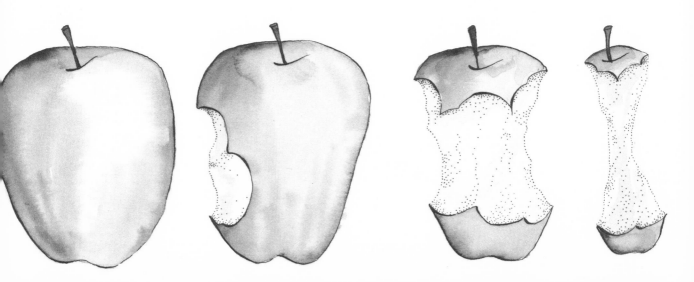

Take One

      old apple tree   and climb and shake
      and pick enough apples    to fill one
large
      grocery bag
              then carry them
                        inside
      and begin to work

cut out the core    of seeds
cut the apples in half
cut out the worms and bugs
                 peel and slice
                   thin

then follow your best family recipe  for pie
or cobbler or tarts or cake or crisp    or pie
or crunch or turnovers or dumplings or pie

get help on everything but the eating

At The End Of Summer

>                    when the old tree   is full
>                    and leaning to the ground
>                    with its heavy load

i pledge my loyalty
>                    to apple pie
>                              and

i insist on deep
>          done dough
as heavy as gold
as golden
>          as sweet sun
>                    and
>                              no other
>          of this
>                    natural   world

unless

there is a peach or rhubarb national
emergency    or mince and pumpkin flooding
in the fall    and the president calls
to ask

will you please do your share
and eat for dear america

wild berry in the spring    chocolate
cream    or boston dream and
all

the other flavors that
wake

me shaking in the night
are

only tasty second best

until

each end of summer
when i pledge

my loyalty again to
apple

only

and always

apple

Grandma Ida$_s$ Cookie Dough For Apple Pie Crust

mix in a large bowl    ½ cup sugar
                                    ½ cup oil
                                    2 eggs                until they are creamed

add    2 tablespoons orange juice
          ½ teaspoon vanilla                and stir well

sift together    2½ cups flour
                          2 teaspoons baking powder
                                                            and
add this flour combination to the
creamy liquid    but do it slow    then stir until you have
                                                            a soft ball of dough

cover with a kitchen towel and place in refrigerator
          from 2 to 12 hours    until you are ready for pie
then grease and flour a pan    spread out half of the dough
          ball until you have a bottom crust for your pie

or you can flour a board and roll out the dough to make
          two crusts    a bottom is a bottom    but a top can
          be strips of dough    or one whole crust

just    get your apples and begin

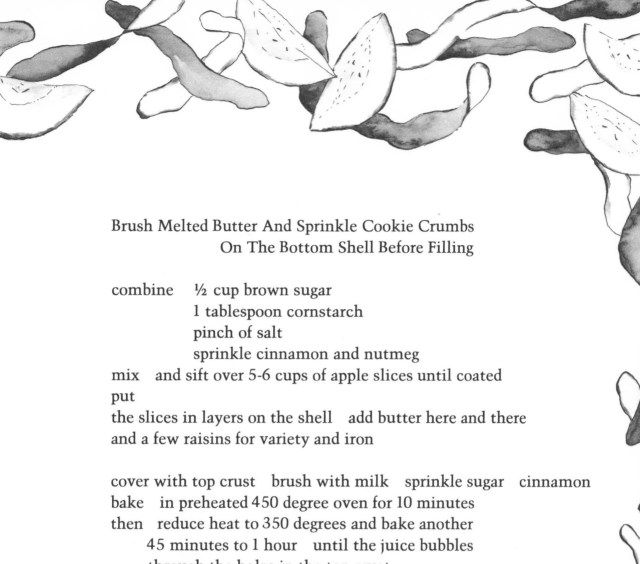

Brush Melted Butter And Sprinkle Cookie Crumbs
        On The Bottom Shell Before Filling

combine    ½ cup brown sugar
           1 tablespoon cornstarch
           pinch of salt
           sprinkle cinnamon and nutmeg
mix   and sift over 5-6 cups of apple slices until coated
put
the slices in layers on the shell   add butter here and there
and a few raisins for variety and iron

cover with top crust   brush with milk   sprinkle sugar   cinnamon
bake   in preheated 450 degree oven for 10 minutes
then   reduce heat to 350 degrees and bake another
      45 minutes to 1 hour   until the juice bubbles
      through the holes in the top crust
                        and the smell
o the smell

Thank You

        after the buds and the blossoms
      and the apples grown full of juice
   you
   can   on an august morning   after your
                  belly is full

   give the old tree a hug

Hard

is
in
  the
middle
   of
    a
carrot
   on
    a
loose

tooth

Soft

is
on
  a
  bed
with
book
a
pillow
for my
head
   and
quiet

Raisins
  in
   one
hand

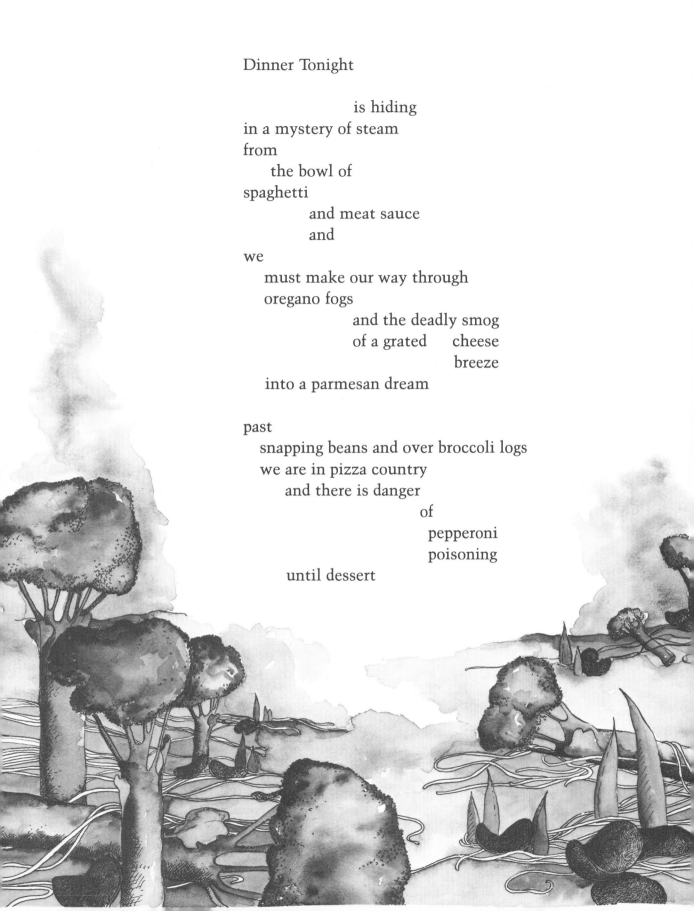

Dinner Tonight

                is hiding
in a mystery of steam
from
    the bowl of
spaghetti
        and meat sauce
        and
we
    must make our way through
    oregano fogs
          and the deadly smog
        of a grated     cheese
                breeze
    into a parmesan dream

past
    snapping beans and over broccoli logs
    we are in pizza country
      and there is danger
                of
                pepperoni
                poisoning
      until dessert

The Baker

           wanted me to know
that
    underneath   the cheese
                 and
    sausage bits
            and
    pepperoni
      slices    and beneath the onions
            and mushrooms and green
                      pepper
                       dices
the only thing that counted
was
the
    dough

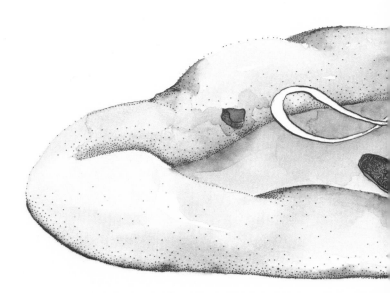

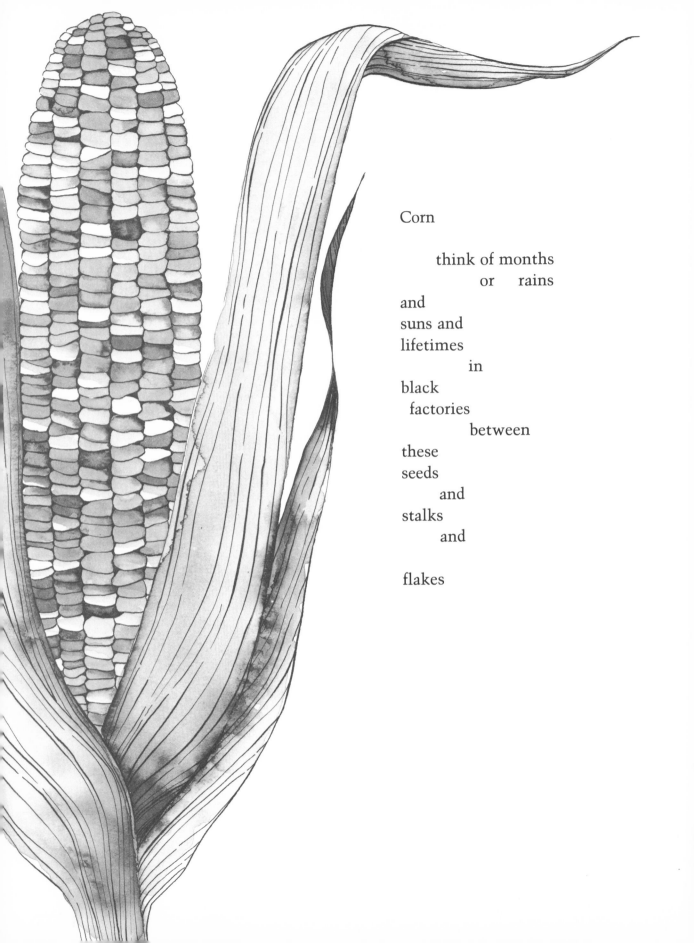

Corn

think of months
or       rains
and
suns and
lifetimes
in
black
factories
between
these
seeds
and
stalks
and

flakes

Burger

       back
        up
seven
spaces
        into
         my
mouth
       do
       not
pass

        go

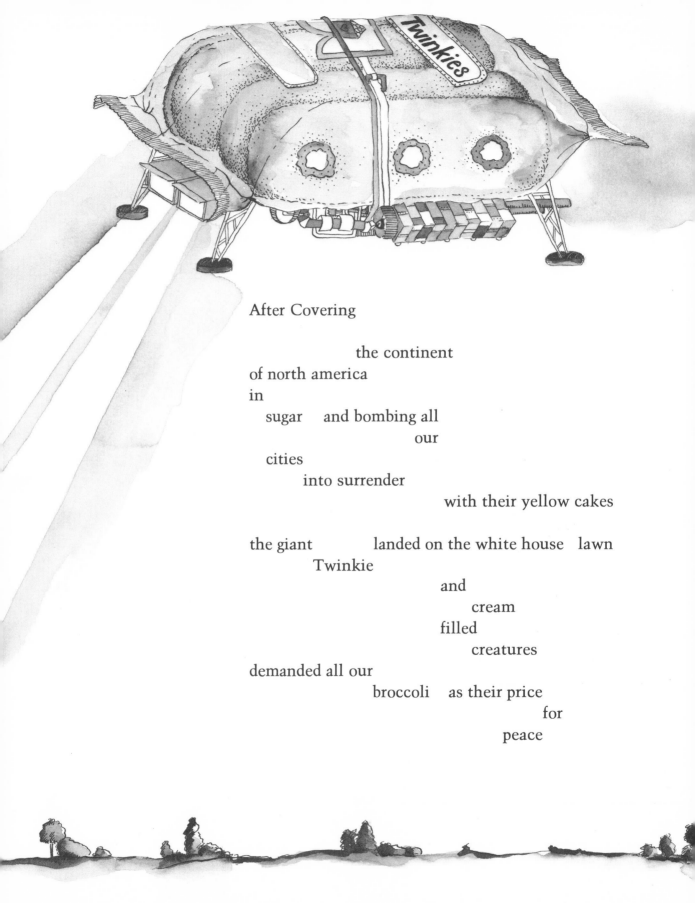

After Covering

                        the continent
of north america
in
    sugar    and bombing all
                        our
    cities
            into surrender
                            with their yellow cakes

the giant            landed on the white house    lawn
            Twinkie
                            and
                                cream
                            filled
                                creatures
demanded all our
            broccoli    as their price
                                    for
                        peace

Sun Flowers

              they are so beautiful
in perfect
          circle
          rows
inside
        their collars of green
              leaves

        we hate to pick
            their seeds
                out
                for
        the oven pan

they will roast
        slowly
and
dry   to the
         taste
     of autumn
sun

Cut
Out

an ugly face    with triangle eyes
and a big    tooth    mouth    for the
                    candle    glow
then scrape the seeds
                out
                and
wash them
        and put them
in a flat and shallow
                pan
in a low oven
        for as long as you can wait
                this dark night

when they are done baking
                you
                    eat
            be fore
            booing

Under

      this autumn sky    i think of these
      ingredients when they were rooted
      in the ground
                that pound of flour
                              as
      some stalks
                of wheat
    this sugar as
            sweet
      sugar canes or beets

      even the chicken eggs
      and salt and rising
                yeast

i always use this wooden spoon to stir
            the batter for the bread
it was
      once a tree    or part of a tree
           rooted in the ground
under
    the
    sky

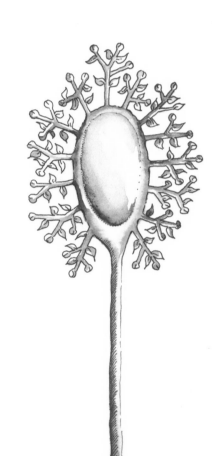

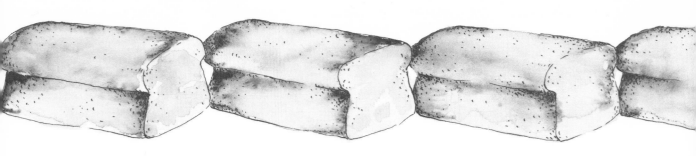

Turn The Oven On

                            To 350 Degrees     and Grease
                          A Deep And Round Baking Pan

first    combine in a large bowl    2 cups unsifted flour
                                      2 envelopes dry yeast
                                      1 tablespoon salt
                                      ¼ cup sugar

then    heat in a small pot
                              1 cup milk
                              1 cup water
                              ¼ cup oil
until you have a warm liquid
                that is not too hot

                mix this warm liquid    and 2 eggs
                        into the flour combination
blend
until the yeast is dissolved

use a wooden spoon to stir into the bowl
                another 2½ cups of flour
then keep stirring until you have a bowl
                          of stiff batter

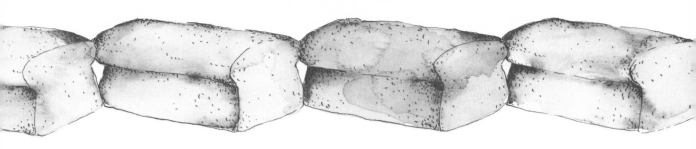

Cover The Bowl With A Kitchen Towel

put in a warm place    and let the dough rise
for an hour    then stick your wooden spoon
into the dough and stir it down    and spoon
                              it into your pan

bake for 45 minutes   until the loaf begins to brown
then
take it out of the oven and brush on an Egg Wash or
                                        Dorure
              of    1 egg yolk
                              beaten with
                2 tablespoons of milk
                    and a pinch of salt
then
bake again until golden brown

              remove from oven

                        cool
                    down

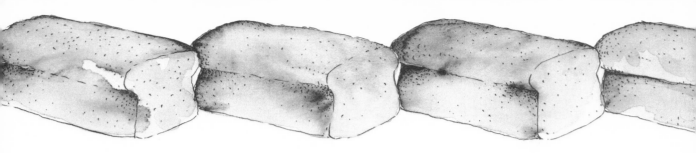

Good For The Head

                        when you need more
                                    sleep
but
you are sitting at the breakfast
        table
            instead
not
    ready for school

                        some quiet
                            cream
                      of
                      peanut
                       butter
on a piece
             of
natural
        brown
         bread

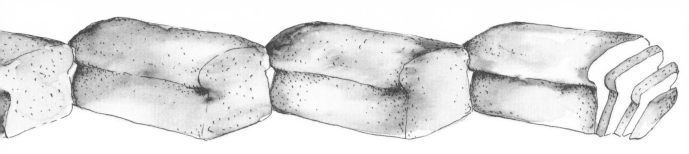

Peanut Butter Batter Bread

mix in a large bowl    1 cup unsifted flour
                                   ½ cup instant oats
                                   ½ cup yellow cornmeal
                                   ½ cup sugar
                                   ½ cup powdered milk
                                   3 teaspoons baking powder
                                   1 teaspoon salt


when they are all stirred together well
      add 2/3 cup peanut butter (either kind)
      and combine until the pieces are small
then
beat 2 eggs and 1½ cups milk (liquid)
      add to flour mixture    stir well
pour
into greased and floured 9x5x3 bread pan

bake in preheated 325 degree oven for an hour

remove   cool   spread   eat

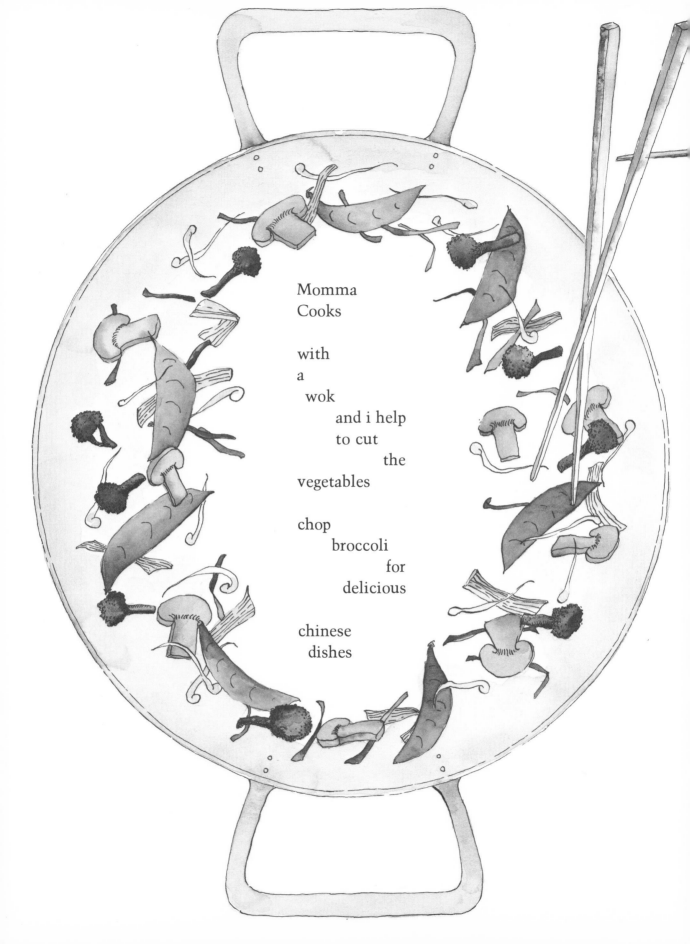

Momma
Cooks

with
a
　wok
　　　and i help
　　　to cut
　　　　　the
vegetables

chop
　　broccoli
　　　　for
　　delicious

chinese
dishes

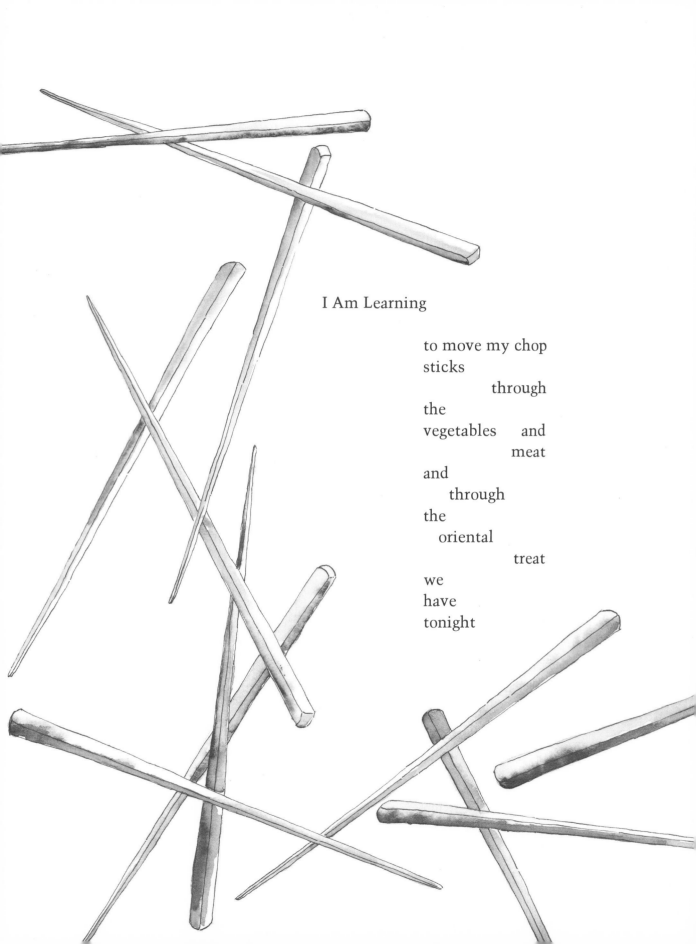

I Am Learning

to move my chop
sticks
              through
the
vegetables    and
              meat
and
      through
the
    oriental
             treat
we
have
tonight

but    in
between
    my
    smiles
   and
    bites
i
write
a
message
    in
    the
sweet
   and
sour
pork

i
need
a
 fork

Deep Into Winter

                    before the January thaw
when the snow
                is a foot high     in our field
                and crusted   with thick ice
and
the berries are gone from the buckthorn
                                and wild rose


the rabbits begin to eat the bark of young        trees
     the yellow apple   the korean cherry bushes
                        and even the redbud saplings
leaving long tooth circles around their trunks


stopping to chew and listen
                                their famous ears
                            are straight up
their noses     point to the safety of the hedge


their eyes in our direction

Just

      when winter spreads out
      across the fields     and it is colder
than    we remember cold

here
come    tangerines   rolling up from Florida
onto    the market shelves
                an orange army

almost
      by themselves
they
      are
      the
        seeds of spring

There Is A Place

on
the couch
        for
        grandma
and
a place on
        grandma
for
  me

  in front
of
the
  fire
    and pop
        ping
        corn

The Coach Said

i had

the

youngest
roundest

belly

he

had  ever  felt

was

un

nec

ess

ary

for basketball

The New Pants

                i found
under the
        christmas
             tree
two
  weeks
ago

are hardly worn
but
     split on me
           yesterday
as
i caught the long bomb
and was trying
        to
        go
all
the
way

I Love To Eat        I Love To Eat
              What

and
i love to eat   a lot
        of all
        of that
                but
i am
        growing tall
                not
                    fat
and my
    eyes are almost to the shelf
        my hands can reach
                            for
                        the
        extra treats each
                        after
                    noon

soon
        i will be grown